Anxiety In Rel

GW00393213

CONFIDENT LOVE

Leave Fear In The Past And
Become The Man You Know
You Can Be

Lance Luna

Table of Contents

Chapter 1:

10 Thoughts That Can Destroy Relationships

You might enjoy the beauty and joy that comes with being in a loving and committed relationship, but it's not always butterflies and beds of roses. It's ubiquitous for you or your partner to transform your insecurities into fears and negative thoughts, but they don't treat you right; they may take a toll on your relationship. Negative thoughts may turn into negative actions, which can lead to unhealthy communication, and could impact how you start seeing your significant other. If you relate to any of the below thoughts, it might be time to reevaluate your relationship and how you view the situation.

1. **They don't love me anymore:**

Although it's pretty common to worry about whether the sparks of love are still alive in your partner's heart or not, constantly asking them whether they still love you might do more harm than good. It could stir up a lot of conflicts based on your insecurities and fears. Even if your partner reassures you by saying that they love you, it could put them in doubt as to there must be a matter causing these concerns. Instead of swinging and jumping to conclusions, communicate effectively with your partner in a way that's suitable for both of you.

2. The power word "should":

It is more or less a major red flag to not tell your partner about what you're thinking rather than automatically assuming that they should know how to read your mind. Blaming your partner for understanding the things that are affecting you secretly, like, "he should know how much it bothers me when he doesn't give me time" or "she should understand how busy i am these days" isn't fair at all. You should be able to voice all your frustrations but in a way that you make your partner understand and not push them away.

3. The blame game:

It's easier to point fingers at your partner and blame them for your spoiled mood rather than taking actions against yourself. Blaming them only postpones any improvements that are needed in your relationship. Instead, try talking to them about it. Tell them when they are wrong and apologize for something that you did to hurt them. We can never predict or control others' emotions, but we can very well hold our own.

4. Overactive imagination:

This mostly happens when you're overthinking about a situation and jump straight to conclusions without having any actual evidence. For instance, if your partner is coming home late at night and they're telling you it's because of the heavy workload, you automatically assume it's because they're having an affair and they're lying to you. These may happen when you have a piece of unattended emotional baggage from previous relationships. It's important to understand that you know your partner well, and they will never do such a thing to hurt you. Have a conversation with your partner about this and seek reassurance if needed.

5. Comparing and contrasting:

You start to put your partner under the pressure of unrealistic expectations when you compare them with a person you see as ideal. For example, if you met your best friend's boyfriend and witnessed an action they did, and you wished that your boyfriend should do the same, you might be disrespecting your partner by asking them to change into who they aren't. It's unhealthy to put that sort of pressure on them. Instead, ask your partner politely if they're willing to do that for you since you liked a particular quality or trait in a person, but you should also tell them that they are lovable regardless.

6. Fantasizing:

Unless you are in a toxic relationship, reminiscing and fantasizing about someone other than your partner might badly affect your relationship. It's because you will keep thinking about the possibilities of being with someone else rather than working on the flaws of your relationship. This might destroy your relationship in ways you can't even imagine.

7. All or nothing:

Seeing your partner as a perfect human being without mistakes, flaws, or imperfections is an idea for destruction. Having extreme thoughts that they can do no wrong or thinking that they always do the wrong thing can mess up with your own and your partner's mental health. Try accepting their failures and mistakes, and keep in mind that, like you, they're just ordinary human beings.

8. Label slinging:

Constantly putting labels on your partner, like calling them lazy when they couldn't complete their chores or calling them insensitive if they don't address a particular issue, may cause problems in your relationship. Instead, we should try to see the positive things in them and help them improve themselves.

9. You think you can't compete with their ex:

Their ex is their ex for a reason. Constantly trying to be like them and asking about them isn't helpful in any way; it can make your relationship weak and your partner frustrated.

10. You think that you're hard to love:

Worrying about pushing your partner away while addressing your insecurities is normal, but that doesn't in any way mean that you're hard to love. Everyone is special and unique in their tracks and can be loved by their partner no matter what.

Conclusion:

While these thoughts might be the perfect recipe to destroy your relationship, a little effort, and hard work into it can go a long way and save your relationship.

Chapter 2:

What To Do When You Have Thoughts of Breaking Up

It's not always easy deciding if you should break up with your partner: You probably care about them and have many great memories together. But there could be real issues in the relationship that make you wonder if it's best to end things. Whatever outcome you settle on, however, it's a good idea to first ask yourself a few questions so you can be sure it's the right decision for you.

"Breaking up with your partner is the best thing to do if you feel like you're not happy anymore, and the relationship is just pulling you down instead of pushing you up.

Here are some things to think about before ending your relationship, according to experts.

1.Is There Anyone Influencing My Decision?

If you're seriously considering breaking up with your partner, it's wise to take a moment to think about what — or, more specifically, who — might be influencing you toward this decision. Is your mom insisting you'd be better off without them? Does your best friend swear that splitting up is your best option? Although people's opinions can be a good guiding force, at the end of the day, this is your choice, not theirs.

2. Do We Hold the Same Core Values?

When you and your partner first got together, you might have initially bonded because you have similar interests. But if you're now at a place where you're thinking of taking the next steps or breaking up, it's worth asking yourself if the two of you align on values, too. "Preferences in daily life will change, but core values will likely not change. "You could feel like it is time to break up with your partner because those [incompatible] core values are showing themselves."

3. Would I Want My Child to Be With Someone Like My Partner?

It may seem like a strange thing to consider if starting a family isn't on the horizon, but it can be an effective litmus test to picture how you'd feel if your child were with someone like your partner. "This will trigger a reality check — would you want your children to spend the rest of their lives with the same kind of person as your partner? "If your answer is no, then take it as a sign that you are heading in the right direction ending the relationship."

4. Is This A Pattern for Me?

Are you someone who starts thinking of breaking up with your partner a few months in each time you're in a relationship? Do you start losing interest at about the one-year mark? Ask yourself whether this is a genuine impulse or if it's just a pattern for you. "Is the reason I desire to break up with someone unique to this person, or would it apply to multiple people?" Clara Artschwager, "If it applies to more than one person, this is often indicative of a larger limiting pattern in relationships."

Are you scared of getting too close to someone? Are you afraid of commitment? Reflecting on these things can help with your decision.

Chapter 3:

7 Ways To Live Together In Harmony With Your Partner

A harmonious relationship can make a person's life happy and beautiful, but, unfortunately, not all of us are blessed with a harmonious relationship. It is essential to work on your relationship in order to make it work. Creating a harmonious bond between you and your partner can make your relationship more healthy and stable. The dream relationship of everybody is to feel loved, accepted, and respected but to achieve such a relationship, and you need to first work on yourself. You need to make sure that you are doing your best at making your partner feel loved.

Most people nowadays want to find their soulmates, but even when they see their soulmates, they don't have a peaceful relationship; the lack of harmony causes this.

Here are 7 ways to live together in harmony with your partner.

1. Accept Your Partners The Way They Are

The first step to a harmonious relationship is acceptance. It would be best to accept your partners the way they are; distancing them from yourself because of a simple mistake can lead to a toxic relationship. If you choose to love a person and be with them, you need to accept the good and bad in them. As they say that no one is perfect, we all are a work in progress. When you cannot receive your partner the way they are, a harmonious relationship cannot be achieved. It would help if you allowed them to evolve and support them throughout this journey.

2. Be Gentle And Compassionate

When you embody gentleness and compassion, your relationship bond deepens, and there is harmony in the relationship. Instead of jumping to conclusions and reacting dramatically, you need to respond with gentleness and understand your partner's feelings.

Compassion brings grace to a person. To achieve a harmonious relationship, you should give your partner grace to work on themselves, understand, and give them space to evolve and mature. It may take time, but it strengthens a relationship.

3. Expectations Should Be Released

With expectations comes disappointment. Expectations are the unspoken standards you expected your partner to live up to. When your partner does not live up to your expectations, you might feel upset or disappointed, but how can you have such high expectations from your partner about things that are unspoken. Work on letting go of these ideals that the society and your subconscious mind created about how a relationship should be. Release the attachment to situations turning out a specific way. Brace yourself for different outcomes of different situations. Don't expect too much from your partner because your partner, like you, cannot always live up to your expectation.

4. Personal Space In A Relationship

Every human being needs personal space; we often see couples that are always together. It may feel exciting and comforting at first, but everyone needs their personal space to think and function properly. After being with each other with no personal space, one can start feeling suffocated and may behave negatively. It would help if you had time to breathe, to expand, and to look within. To evolve, you need space. Personal space between couples proves that their relationship is healthy and robust.

5. Honesty

Honest communication is not just a factor to achieve a harmonious relationship but also to have any relationship at all. Not being truthful can cause conflicts and problems in a relationship. Moreover, being a liar can be a toxic trait that can cause your partner to end the relationship. But before being honest with your partner, you need to be honest with yourself. Know your true self, explore the good and bad in yourself. Don't hide your mistakes from your partner; instead, be honest and apologize to them before it is too late. Honesty is a crucial factor in achieving a harmonious relationship.

6. Shun Your Ego

Ego and harmony cannot simply go hand in hand; where ego exists, harmony cannot be established. Often by some people, ego is considered a toxic trait. This is the ego that stops a person from apologizing for his mistakes, which can create tension among the couple. The stubbornness to do things your way is caused by ego and can easily result in unwanted scenarios. These are not the components of a healthy relationship. So to establish a harmonious relationship, you should remove ego and learn to compromise a bit. By removing ego, you allow yourself to be more flexible and understanding.

7. Let Go if Unnecessary Emotional Pain

When you keep hurting over old resentments, you convert that pain into toxic feelings that are not good for a relationship. These poisonous feelings can make you make some bad decisions that may result in your partner feeling unsafe around you. This pain can cause you to bury your positives feeling inside. As a result of this, you may feel pessimistic and may exaggerate minor conflicts into something more. A person must let go of this emotional stress and pain. You can let go by going to a therapist or yoga and meditation. Once you have let go of the pain, your heart is now open to a peaceful and harmonious relationship.

To establish a harmonious relationship, you have to accept and understand your partner and work on yourself. Also, work on your radical integrity.

Chapter 4:

Ten Signs You're Falling In Love

As our Literature master, Shakespeare, once said, 'A heart to love, and in that heart, courage, to make's love known.'

Ah, love! A four-lettered small word that leaves such a heavy impact on people. Falling in love is nothing short of a beautiful experience, but it can also give you a veritable roller-coaster of emotions. From feeling unsure to terrifying, disgusting, exhilarating, and excited, you might feel it all. If your mobile screen pops up and you're hoping to see their name on the screen, or you're looking for their face in a crowd full of thousands, then you, my child, are doomed! You are well familiar with the feeling of getting butterflies just by hearing their voice, the urge to change your wardrobe completely to impress them, the constant need to be with them all the time. It is known that people who are in love tend to care about the other person's needs as they do their own.

You often go out of their way for their happiness. Whether it's something as small as making their favorite dish or impressing them with some grand gestures, you always try to make them feel content and happy.

If you're in the middle of some casual inquiry into whether you're falling in love, then we are here to help you. Below are some signs for you to discover if it's really just simply a loss of appetite or if you're merely lovesick.

1. **You don't hesitate to try new things with them:**

One of the factors that you could look into is that you become fearless and more adventurous when you are in love. You don't hang back to step out of your comfort zone and engage in all your partner favors' activities and interests. Suddenly the idea of trying sushi or wearing something bright doesn't seem so crazy. You are willing to be more daring and open to new experiences. You are ready to go on that spontaneous trip with them and make memories, all while being a little scared inside. But isn't love all about trying new things with your partner? The New York Times article in 2008 revealed that people in a relationship who try new hobbies together help keep the spark alive long after the honeymoon phase is over.

2. You're always thinking about them:

When you are in love, you always tend to think about your partner. Rehash your last conversation with them, or simply smiling at something they said, or questions like what they must be doing right now, have they eaten their meal yet, did they go to work on time or were late again, are always on the back of your mind. You are mentally, emotionally, and physically impacted about caring for them. But it isn't overwhelming. Instead, you get a sense of a calm and secure reality that you will constantly crave. When in love, we tend to merge with that person in such a way that they start to dominate our thoughts and we become wholly preoccupied with them.

3. You become anxious and stressed:

According to a psychology study, falling in love could also cause higher levels of cortisol, a stress home, in your body. So the next time you feel jittery or anxious, that person might mean more to you than you think. You might become anxious to dress up nicely to impress them, or if they ask you something, the pressure of answering them intellectually can be expected. But suppose you're feeling overly anxious about your partner, like them not texting you back instantly or thinking they might be cheating on you. In that case, it's an indication of insecure attachment, and you might want to work on yourself to avoid feeling like this.

4. You become inspired and motivated:

A few days ago, you needed the motivation to get out of bed. And now, the future suddenly seems so bright and full of potential. Your partner inspires you to set up new goals, have a positive attitude, and cheer you from behind while you feel full of energy and chase them. When we are in love, a part of our brain, considered the reward system, releases excess dopamine, and we feel invincible, omnipotent, and daring. Your life becomes significantly better when you're around them.

5. You become empathetic towards them:

It's not a secret that you start seeing your partner as an extension of yourself and reciprocate whatever they feel when you fall in love. Suppose they are accepted into their favorite program, or they expect to receive that interview call, or their favorite football team might have lost in the quarters. In that case, you might feel the same excitement, happiness, or distress that your partner does. Becoming empathetic towards your partner means making sacrifices for them, like going to the grocery store because your partner is tired or refueling their tank in the cold so that they don't have to step out. According to an expert, "Your love is growing when you have an increased sense of empathy toward your partner. When they feel sad, you feel sad. When they feel happy, you feel happy. This might mean going out of the way to give them love in the way that they want to receive it, even if it is not the way you would want to receive love."

6. It's just plain easy:

You don't have to put in extra effort, and it doesn't seem to drain your energy. Instead, you feel energized and easy. You can be your complete, authentic self around them. And it always just seems to go with the flow. Even the arguments don't feel much heated as they did in the other relationships. When you're in love, you prioritize your partner over your pride and ego. You don't hesitate to apologize to them and keep your relationship above everything. When you are with your partner, and it doesn't feel like hard work, know that they are the one!

7. You crave their presence:

Some theorists say that we are more drawn to kissing, hugging, and physical touch when we fall in love. Physical closeness releases a burst of the love hormone termed Oxytocin, which helps us feel bonded. Of course, you don't want to come as someone too clingy who is permanently attached to his partner's hip, but knowing where your person is or how their day went is what you should be looking forward to. On the flipside, Corticotrophin is released as part of a stress response when we are away from our partner, which can contribute to anxiety and depression.

8. You feel safe around them:

It takes a lot of courage for people to open up to their partners. If you don't mind being vulnerable around them, or if you've opened up to them about your dark past or addressed your insecurities, and they have listened contently to you and reassured you. You have done vice versa with your partner, then that's just one of the many signs that you both are in love with each other. Long-lasting love gives you a solid ground and a safe space where you can be upset and vulnerable. When we feel an attachment to our partner, our brain releases the hormones vasopressin and Oxytocin, making us feel secure.

9. You want to introduce them to your family and friends:

You just never shut up about your love interest over the family dinner or when hanging out with your friends. They know all about them, from their favorite spot in the city to the color of their eyes, to how much you adore them and want to spend every single minute talking about them. And now all your family members and friends are curious to meet the guy/girl they have been listening about for the past few weeks. You want to introduce them into every aspect of your life and want it to last this time. So, you make perfect arrangements for them to meet your friends and family, and on the other hand, threatens them to behave Infront of him/her.

10. You care about their happiness:

When you put them and their feelings first, that's how you know it's true love. You don't just want happiness for yourself only, but instead wants it in excess measure for your partner. According to marriage researchers at UC Berkeley, " Spouses who love each other stay together longer, be happier, and support each other more effectively than couples who do not love each other compassionately." You want to go out of your way, or do their favorite thing, to see a smile on their face.

Conclusion:

If you relate to the signs above, then you've already been hit by the love cupid. Scientists have discovered that falling in love, is in fact, a real thing. The brain releases Phenylethylamine, a hormone known for creating feelings of infatuation towards your significant other. The mix and match of different hormones released in our body while we are in love are wondrous. If you have gotten lucky and found a special someone for yourself, then cling to them and don't let them go! If you found this video helpful, please like and subscribe to the channel. Also don't forget to share this video with someone who you find might benefit from this topic as well!

Chapter 5:

10 Signs You've Outgrown Your Friendship

There is almost no one in this world that doesn't have a friend. Some of us even have ten best friends. It all depends on two factors. First is that you have to pick a type of friend and second one is that you find them in this life. Mostly everyone has. Since childhood, you might have had lots of friends. But, did they stay? We eventually have to leave them behind even if we don't want to. It's important to know when to leave them behind, and here are ten signs that you've outgrown your friendship.

1. You disregard them:

When you've outgrown your friendship with someone, you ignore them. You forget spending time with them. It is unhealthy for a company to disregard each other in any way. So, you naturally drive apart from them. You start to choose different places to hang instead of hanging around with them like you used to.

2. You pretend:

When you are with a friend, all you want is to be yourself. And when you feel like you need to pretend like someone else or like your old self, that's a red flag. You might not fall into each other's expectations of grownups. And it disappoints you both. Compatibility is a key to friendship.

3. Lack of effort:

Friendship has to grow in the right places, and if it doesn't, then it's not meant to work out. When there are no efforts from even one side, then you both will break apart. One-sided friendship is draining and tiring. We might be ghosting them without even noticing, so it is always better to cut them off.

4. You get awkward around each other:

One thing that is the most wondrous about friendship is that you can be comfortable around each other even in silence. If you are finding that peaceful silence awkward, then it's an outgrown friendship. It will only make this friendship a burden to you and them. Getting out of this tricky situation means getting out of your company with them.

5. You have nothing to discuss:

Communication is what makes a friendship stronger. When you got nothing to talk about, then you don't have to talk to them at all. There is always something to talk about, and it only depends on the person we are willing to tell. You need to find a person that you want to listen to you.

6. You both are going different ways:

Life takes everyone on a different path. When you and your friend choose other ways, then it's natural for you to weaken your bond with each other. You both will make new friends according to your phases in life, and that is not such a bad deal. Letting go would be healthy in this situation and for your good.

7. Support is unequal:

Supporting each other is extremely important in friendship. And if you or your friend doesn't have this quality, you are not a good match. Sometimes, in times of need. That's all that one wants. Advice in this situation may seem like disagreeing.

8. You keep secrets:

Sharing your day, feelings, and thoughts with your friends sounds like a regular activity for all of us. But some might not agree. When you start to keep things from each other, then that is your weak spot. That is the time you should realize that they are just there for a tag of friend and not playing the actual part.

9. You don't understand each other anymore:

One of the things that keeps a friendship strong is the compatible understanding between the two of you. And if one of you fails to understand the other one, then you've outgrown your company. It's the aspect that completes you both, and without it, you both are just on loose ends.

10. You don't have any more familiar grounds:

It was the mutual interest in certain things that bought you two close enough to be friends. Eventually, you both will find different things likable. Your friend might hate those things and never tell you. But when you sit together and find nothing to talk about. That is where you have to end this friendship.

Conclusion:

Friends might have a significant impact on our lives, but we have to let them go eventually. You will make lots of friends along the way. Leaving one behind doesn't make you the wrong person. It makes you strong one.

Chapter 6:

6 Steps To Recover From A Breakup

Breakups are tough to go through. Even when they end with good terms, it still brings out many insecurities and traumas of the past. These include the fear of abandonment, loneliness, etc. Breakups have become a prevalent thing for us, so familiar that we sometimes forget how painful it can be. When you have imagined your whole future with someone, and someone ends up leaving you, you feel broken, but you would know it happened for a reason. Recovering from a breakup is not an impossible thing to do, and most of us recover from a partition even if it may take some time. Here are a few steps to recover from a breakup.

1. Talk About It

After a breakup, everything seems to be falling apart, and it is tough to talk about it, about the pain it has caused. But it is scientifically proven that talking about your breakup helps you recover from it; as you start talking about it, you are reminded about what went wrong. This enables you to understand that it was for good. When you talk about it to others, they tell you their perspective, and you start to see things from a different point of view; this way, you understand what went wrong, and you begin to feel more okay with things.

2. Keep A Journal

Even though talking helps, sometimes we can't find the right person to talk to, who will understand us. In a situation like this, you can always start journaling; it is an emotional release, where you write about your feelings, where you pour your heart out. You will feel more comfortable because no one will judge you; as you start writing, your hands would automatically write something that would surprise you, but those surprising things will help you figure yourself out.

3. Write Again and Again

When journaling, act as if you are telling all these things to a stranger and don't stop just then, write again and again as if you are talking to a different stranger every time you write about your breakup, it will help you gain a different perspective, you would realize many things, but above all, you would learn that whatever happened, happened for a better tomorrow.

4. Let It All Out

When going through a breakup, we all want to scream, shout and let all the anger out, but of course, you can't do all these things in public. So take some time out for yourself, go somewhere private, and talk all the anger, frustration, and tears out. It is normal to feel this way after a breakup, but remember that bottling up your emotions is never good. On the other hand, letting it all out helps you a lot; this would reduce the pressure of all your feelings.

5. Stick To Your Routine

When going through a hard time, we stop following our daily routine, sure it is okay to take some time off from work, but it is not okay to stop eating. When going through a heartbreak, many people stop eating correctly, start sleeping more in the mornings, and just kind of mess their routine. But now is the time to work on yourself, don't stop eating healthy, don't mess up your sleeping habits, and above all, start going to the gym; you can let all the anger and frustration out through some exercise.

6. It Is Time To Make Yourself Feel Special

After a breakup, your sense of self-worth is reduced, a lot of insecurities attack you, but this is not the time to hate yourself; it is the time to love yourself. Don't just sit at home, watching a movie and crying about your breakup; what you can do is get a change. You can go shopping, buy new clothes, jewelry, etc. Get a new haircut, and love the new you. Focus on yourself, become selfish for a while. Now you don't have to think about anyone else, set new goals, and above all, take care of yourself.

Conclusion

Breakups have become very common, so familiar that people sometimes forget what it feels like, but don't worry, and you were not born with this person, try to work on yourself and give yourself the love you deserve. Remember that you are worth someone who cares about you and loves you the way you want to be loved. It is okay to be single; it is the time to try new things and redefine yourself.

Chapter 7:

7 Reasons Why Men Cheat

Men and women may cheat for different reasons, but it's likely due to the way men and women are socialized rather than any innate differences between them. The more we, as a society, move away from socialization and patriarchy, the less we see those gender differences in cheating behavior. However, nonetheless, research shows that men are more likely to cheat than women. The ratio is 20% of men have admitted to cheating compared to 13% of women.

We should never forget that our minds are more resilient than we give them credit for. Cheating in a relationship is solely that person's fault, no matter the circumstances. It can always be avoided if the person wants to. There are many reasons why men cheat, along with what defines cheating and signs to watch out for. Here are some reasons and behaviors that might apply to people of all genders but could be relevant to men.

1. They're Looking For A Way Out

Sometimes the first step for a man to get out of a relationship is to cheat. Although people of all genders might cheat, for this reason, men are most likely to do it. This is because men are less likely to have difficult conversations with their partners and seldom tell their own needs in a relationship. So, they see cheating as the only way out. Instead of having to bear the difficult conversation with their partner when they're done with their relationship, they escape through it all by the act of cheating and having an affair.

2. They're Looking For A Connection

Cheating doesn't always happen for physical reasons only, despite what gender norms might tell us about men. Feeling unseen, unheard, or disconnected from their partners can also contribute as a factor for it. Men are much less likely to have a sound social support system, and those things can hurt and make them go into a zone where they feel protected. In those instances, if a woman shows compassion and support, they welcome her with open arms. It might start with a friendship with someone who will make him feel better about himself, and hence, an emotional connection forms.

3. They Have Sociopathic or Narcissistic Traits

If a partner has cheated, there could be more than just finding a way out of their relationship. There can be narcissistic tendencies or sociopathic traits involved. They could be someone who doesn't care about their partner's feelings, and they might do it simply because they want to. When an opportunity to cheat presents itself, they go towards it without giving a damn about their partner.

4. Revenge Cheating

Some people act on their impulses and cheat out of anger, jealousy, or desire revenge. It's not necessary that their partner might have cheated on them; even if they have done something slight to upset them (like having a close friendship with another man), they'll end up cheating on their partner to make a point.

5. Struggles With Substance Abuse

Cheating becomes more likely if one is dealing with a substance abuse problem. Substance addiction can create an impulse-driven and more immature version of ourselves. Many relationships tend to fall apart if one of the two partners has become addicted to a substance and acts subconsciously on their impulse.

6. They Seek Validation

If someone is not getting validation in their relationship, then insecurity and low self-esteem can drive them to cheat. If they don't feel attracted enough to their partner, they may cheat to seek external validation. Sexual issues can also cause someone to look for someone newer to prove themselves to.

7. They're Emotionally Immature

Emotional immaturity is sometimes the core of why men cheat. Since childhood, men are expected and taught not to talk about their feelings and emotions. This inability to speak leads to several issues and conflicts in their relationships. By the time you know it, they are having an affair and cheating on their significant other. Cheating can be an essential consequence of poor judgment, lack of willpower, self-control, and immaturity. A mature man will always talk about his feelings and resolve conflicts and issues with his partner.

Conclusion:

Being cheated on can be the worst trauma anyone can experience, and there can be so many reasons it might have happened in different relationships and contexts. But no matter the reason, it cannot be denied that infidelity forces both of you to step back. Analyze what went wrong and decide how you both want to move forward from there.

Chapter 8:

How To Survive a Long Distance Relationship

Today we're going to talk about a very touchy yet important subject. If you have a partner who's not local, or you know that they are going to move countries some day, you've gotta be prepared for that time to come. You've got to be sure whether you will begin a long distance relationship or whether you will move to that country to be with that person.

For the purpose of this video, I am going to assume that you have already committed to being in a long distance relationship. And as with any commitment, you have got to be willing to make compromises and sacrifices to maintain that relationship.

There are a couple of things that you will have to mentally prepare yourself for if you are in it for the long haul with this person. They could be gone for days, weeks, months, or even years. First of all you have to ask yourself, are you okay with seeing this person only once every few months? Will you be happy if you wont be able to spend majority of the time with the person throughout the year? How will you cope with the distance? Are you okay with not having physical intimacy with the person? Will you be willing to sacrifice your freedom to wait for this person to return? And can you trust this person to be faithful to you as you spend all your time apart?

For me personally, I was committed to a Long distance relationship once before. And it was the hardest thing for me to do. Especially when it came time at the airport for the send off.

Having already known prior that it would happen someday, i still went ahead with the relationship. All was well and all was fun, but time soon caught up with us and before i knew it, it was already time to say goodbye... temporarily at least. I must admit that it was tough... It was tough because we have gotten so used to spending time together physically in the same space for so long, that this sudden transition was all foreign territory to me. Not being able to touch each other, not being able to meet up for meals, not being able to just hang out at the movies, and not to mention the time zone difference. These were all very real challenges. And they were incredible hard especially in the first few months. I cried at the airport, i cried on the drive home, I was incredibly unhappy, and i was not prepared in any capacity whatsoever to feel this way. You never really know how to feel about something until it actually happens to you.

Knowing that the next time we would see each other would be months away, there was no way to know how to feel or act when suddenly it feels like a limb has been chopped off and you are just struggling to find your feet again. I looked to friends for social support and that was the thing that got me through the toughest periods. Sure we could still FaceTime and call and whatever. Especially in this day and age, but it was still tough having a relationship over the computer. It does feel like on some level you're dating virtually. Everything had to change and I had to relearn what it meant to be in a relationship all over again. I wasn't ever a sappy or clingy boyfriend. I know that about myself. But I do have an expectation to meet up maybe once or twice in a week. Now it's once or twice a year. And it's not fun at all.

So now I put that question back to you, after hearing this part of the story, are you willing to put yourself through this? Or would it be easier if you just chose someone who is in the same physical space with you with no plans on leaving town. If you were to ask me, I might actually do it all over again with someone like that.

The next thing that you've got to have to survive a long distance relationship, is to have a strong social support group. A group of friends that you can share your troubles with. People who can empathise with you, and people who can spend time with you in lieu of your partner. You never want to be in a situation where your partner is your entire world, because when they leave, you will most likely crumble. If you relied on them for all your happiness, their sudden absence will certainly leave you devastated. If u do not have a strong support network of friends, i would suggest you think doubly hard about committing to a long distance relationship.

Now comes the most important part, in my opinion, of having a successful long distance relationship. And that is trust. Trust in each other to be faithful, and trust in each other to do the right thing at all times.

I will bring back to my experience with my long distance relationship. To keep things short, after about a year into my LDR, i discovered that my partner had been cheating on me many times over. And my whole world did come crashing down. Having thought that everything was going according to plan up until that point, i was completely blindsided by the avalanche that hit me. It really hit me hard. But I knew that i loved myself more, and so I packed my bags and flew back home from the trip.

Getting over the relationship was relatively easy because i knew there was nothing left there anymore. There was no more trust to come home to. I had no faith in the relationship anymore and it was effectively over for me. It may sound too easy watching this video, but trust me i went through a great deal and I was incredibly happy with my decision. I learned that i was incredibly resilient and that even though things didn't work out the way i had hoped, and even though my vision of the future was changed drastically, it didn't knock me down. And I chose myself first.

So my question that I put to you now is, to what extent do you trust your partner to be faithful to you? Has he or she cheated on you before? Have they always chosen you first? Can you touch your heart and say they will never do anything to hurt you? Or are you too naive like I was to believe that all is well? Because I was incredibly confident at one point that we were making the LDR work beautifully. Until it suddenly didn't. Would you be okay if you found out that your partner was cheating on you secretly overseas while you guys were apart? Would you be paranoid of the things he could do? If you can answer these things honestly, then u might be able to LDR make it work for you. If not, again, do reconsider your relationship now.

For me personally, If you don't know my stance by now, I absolutely do not believe in LDR. Especially if it's a permanent period. If your partner is gone maybe for a 3-6 month work trip. Yeah maybe that's doable, but if they are gone for 5-6 years and if there's a big question mark behind that... I would totally back away. It would be a deal breaker for me.

The thing with relationships is that, I believe it is the physical presence, the physical connection, the physical communication, and the physical touch that keeps two people together. Without any of these things on a regular basis, it is likely that a couple with drift apart on some level... And without these things, one might be tempted to seek comfort and physical intimacy elsewhere if they can't wait another 5 months before they can see you again.

But if your foundation is incredibly strong, if you guys have made a commitment, if you guys trust each other completely, and if you believe that your relationship can weather any storm, then I already think that you know you can handle a long distance relationship. I am simply here to affirm to you what you already know.

But take me as a word of warning that even strong relationships do fail in the face of a long distance relationship. So you have to be prepared to handle anything that comes your way.

I hope I have been able to shed some light into this topic for you.

Take care and I'll see you in the next one.

Chapter 9:

8 Signs Someone Misses You

Missing someone can be very painful, almost as if there is something incomplete about your life. You think about them all the time, and the more you try not to think of them, the more you end up doing that. You might find your thoughts wandering and can't seem to focus on anything other than them. You may either find comfort in binge eating or constantly go through their stuff. Well, you're not the only one who might be going through this torture. What if someone is experiencing the same stuff but for you? Here are some signs that tell you someone is missing you.

1. **They keep track of your social media:**

If they haven't unfriended, unfollowed, or blocked you yet, the chances are that they are still keeping track of you. If you find them constantly reacting to your stories, or liking your pictures the minute you put them up, then they're visiting your profile again and again. They have kept their slot open for making a conversation or giving you a hint to try to make conversation with them.

2. Did they find your replacement yet?

For someone ready to move on, it takes a second to find a replacement. If they haven't found one yet, the chances are that they are still reminiscing over you. They're hoping that you'll reconnect and thus, still pine after you. Even if they're hooking up with someone as a rebound, chances are they're doing everything in their power to forget you but are failing miserably.

3. They reach out to you randomly:

Receiving those drunk late-night texts/calls? They're miserable, and all they want to do is talk to you. If they were out there having the time of their life, they wouldn't even remember you let alone bother to text or call you. If they do, it's obviously because you're on their mind and alcohol just gave them a head start to get in touch with you again.

4. Rousing your jealousy so you would notice them:

Have they suddenly started posting a lot about their new life on social media? Chances are they're most certainly trying hard to make you sit up and take notice of them. If they're hanging out with a lot of people that you've never seen or heard of and having a fantastic time, then they're trying to make you jealous.

5. They throw shade at you:

If they're making snide comments or remarks about you or a new partner, they're still clearly hurt and miss you. They might pass a statement on your outfit or your appearance and lash out at you, trying to make you feel as bad as they do. They may also show disapproval of your new date and point out negative things about them. It's clear that they still haven't moved on and clung to that thin thread of hope.

6. They do things to get your attention:

Do they post stuff that points towards you? Or do they write cute love letters or poems mentioning you? This is a pretty obvious sign that they miss you and want to get back in their life. They might also ask your friends about you and crash those uninvited parties because they want to see you. You might also see them around more than usual.

7. They hoard your stuff:

Are they still keeping your shirt/hoodie and making excuses not to give it even when you have asked them a million times? Or are they keeping even the most useless thing that you might have given them years ago? It's probably because they go through this stuff and relive all the old memories associated with them. They're still not ready to give them up and move on.

8. From the horse's mouth:

The most obvious and straightforward sign that someone misses you? They tell you themself! Some people don't like to play games and do unnecessary things to gain your attention or throw hints and clues at you and wait for you to notice them. They tell you straight away that they miss you and they want to do something about it.

Conclusion:

Now that you have all the signs on your plate, it's up to you whether you want to give them a second chance or move on from all of this. The choice is yours!

Chapter 10:

How To Be Your Own Best Friend

Why would you want to become your own best friend? There are several benefits to creating your internal support system rather than relying on your partner, friends, or family to be there for you when you're suffering. Having other people's expectations can lead to disappointment, heartbreak, and relationship breakdown if your expectations aren't met. We all have it in us to give ourselves what we need without seeking it externally.

Of course, it's great if you have a strong support network, but you could still benefit from becoming more self-reliant. And what about if you have no one to turn to for help, or if your current support people are unable to be there for you?

Isn't it far better to know how to support yourself in times of need? Here's how to become your own best friend.

1. Be Nice To Yourself

The first step to becoming a friend is to treat yourself like you would treat a friend. That means that you need to stop being self-critical and beating yourself up. Start by acknowledging your good qualities, talents, and abilities and begin to appreciate your unique self.

When you catch yourself thinking up some nasty self-talk, stop and ask, "Would I say this to my best friend?" If not, then reframe your self-talk to be more supportive and caring.

2. Imagine How You Would Support A Friend In The Same Situation

Think about a loved one, a friend, a family member, someone dear to you and imagine that they are in the same situation you are currently facing. Think about how they're struggling, suffering, and feeling stuck with this problem, then consider how to best offer assistance and advice to them.

Craft the words that you would say to your greatest friend and then say them gently to yourself. Allow yourself to feel supported, and give yourself what you need.

3. Honor Your Needs

Following the theme of considering how you would help a dear friend, **you need to start taking your advice and putting your own needs first**. Do you need a day off from work? A long hot bath? An early night? A wild night? Some time to catch up on your reading, cleaning, gardening, creative projects, social life, or self-care?

Whatever you need, allow yourself to **put it at the top of the list rather than the bottom**. Be there for yourself and make it happen.

4. Send Compassion To The Part of You That is Hurting

Being a friend to yourself involves adopting and mastering the art of self-compassion. Compassion isn't forceful or solution-focused. **Compassion is accepting, peaceful, and loving, without the need to control or change anything**.

Imagine a mother holding a child who has bumped his head. Her compassion is a strong force. She simply holds her child with loving, comforting, gentle arms and whispers, "It will be alright, my love." The child trusts his mother's words just as you learn to trust your own words when speaking to yourself.

Imagine yourself as both the child and the mother simultaneously. Offer compassion at the same time as you open up to receive it.

Use these techniques to become your own best friend and start *being there* **for yourself!**

Chapter 11:

How To Win The Most Attention From Others

Attention. If you only knew how much power attention over someone actually holds. You see, to achieve fame, success, and power, you need to master how to grab someone's attention and never let it go.

The Biggest companies in the world have become so good at this that they are able to hold a command over their most loyal followers by capturing their time and energy into using their products and services. We unknowingly give our time and energy to these great companies because they have mastered the art of taking our attention and never letting go of it. Think of Apple, when they launch a new product, be it an iPhone, ipad, or whatever software and services, almost all the attention and media coverage goes to them. And everyone pays "attention" to what they have to do or say because they hold such an enormous power in the tech industry.

When Princess Diana first graced us in the 1980s, many of us who were still not alive back then, she grabbed the world by storm by always being the Center of attention in all media and news outlets. She had the world in the palm of her hands. The world wanted more of her and all of their attention is spent on watching and analysing her every move. She was the most famous person on Earth for many years right up until her untimely death in 1997.

Fortunately for Princess Diana, she knew how to use the attention while she was alive to good use. She advocated for many humanitarian causes that shed light on issues such as AIDS, landmines, and many issues that were big taboos back then. Whichever causes she dedicated her time to, they benefited from her star power and presence and she lifted many of the stigma associated with it and also helped raise funds for them.

From these two simple examples we now understand how much power attention wields. When you have someone's attention, whether it be 1 person or 1 billion people, you have a hold over them and they will be watching you.

This is why many social media companies are all fighting to get your attention, whether it be through views or paid posts, they want you to be spending time on their platform so that you can spend money with them. That is how they earn their billions from everyone's collective attention.

If you want to be successful in your career or in any aspects of your life, you must learn how draw attention to yourself, in an ethical way, and to use that to your advantage. Those we get promoted faster than their peers would almost always have the attention of their bosses, where they have proven in their abilities and shone louder than their competition and that is why they win. But I want to highlight again that you should do things that help you gain attention ethically.

If you are a business owner, you need to know how to grab the attention of your customers, to be spending more time and money on your products and services. Whether this be done through smart marketing, or word of mouth, you need to draw people's attention to the stuff you are selling. Because even if you have the best product on Earth, it would not be any good if no one is aware of it in the first place.

I challenge each and everyone of you today to find ways that you can draw attention to the areas in your life that feel could use a boost. Come up with solid plans to get more eyeballs looking at you or your products. And i guarantee you that success will come your way a lot sooner.

Chapter 12:

Setting Too High Expectations

Today we're going to talk about the topic of setting too high expectations. Expectations about everything from work, to income, to colleagues, friends, partners, children, family. Hopefully by the end of this video I will be able to help you take things down a notch in some areas so that you don't always get disappointed when things don't turn out the way you expect it to.

Let's go one by one in each of these areas and hopefully we can address the points that you are actively engaged in at the moment.

Let's begin with work and career. Many of us have high expectations for how we want our work life to be. How we expect our companies and colleagues to behave and the culture that we are subjected to everyday. More often that not though, companies are in the business of profit-making and cutting costs. And our high expectations may not meet reality and we might end up getting let down. What I would recommend here is that we not set these expectations of our colleagues and bosses, but rather we should focus on how we can best navigate through this obstacle course that is put in front of us. We may want to focus instead on how we can handle ourselves and our workload. If however we find that we just can't shake off this expectations that we want from working in a company, maybe we want to look elsewhere to companies that have a work culture that suits our personality. Maybe one that is more vibrant and encourages freedom of expression.

Another area that we should address is setting high expectations of our partners and children. Remember that we are all human, and that every person is their own person. Your expectations of them may not be their expectations of themselves. When you impose such an ideal on them, it may be hard for them to live up to. Sure you should expect your partner to be there for you and for your children to behave a certain way. But beyond that everyone has their own personalities and their own thoughts and ideas. And what they want may not be in line with what we want for them. Many a times for Asian parents, we expect our kids to get good grades, get into good colleges, and maybe becoming a doctor or lawyer one day. But how many of us actually understand what our kids really want? How many of us actually listen to what our kids expect of themselves? Maybe they really want to be great at music, or a sport, or even finance. Who's to say what's actually right? We should learn to trust others and let go of some of our own expectations of them and let them become whoever they want to be.

The next area I want to talk about is simply setting too high expectations of yourself. Many times we have an ideal of who we want to be - how we want to look, how we want our bodies to look, and how we want our bank statement to look, amongst many others. The danger here is when we set unrealistic expectations as to when we expect these things to happen. Remember most things in life takes time to happen. The sooner you realise that you need more time to get there, the easier it will be on yourself. When we set unrealistic timelines, while it may seem ideal to rush through the process to get results fast, more often than not we are left disappointed when we don't hit them. We then get discouraged and may even feel like a failure or give up the whole process entirely. Wouldn't it be better if we could give ourselves more time for nature to work its magic? Assuming you follow the steps that you have laid out and the action plans you need to take, just stretch this timeline out a little farther to give yourself more breathing room. If you feel you are not progressing as fast as you had hoped, it is okay to seek help and to tweak your plans as they go along. Don't ever let your high expectations discourage you and always have faith and trust in the process even when it seems hard.

One final thing I want to talk about is how we can shift from setting too high expectations to one of setting far-out goals instead. There is a difference. Set goals that serve to motivate you and inspire you to do things rather than ones that are out of fear. When we say we expect something, we immediately set ourselves up for disappoint. However if we tell ourselves that we really want something, or that we want to achieve something that is of great importance to us, we shift to a goal-oriented mindset. One that is a lot healthier. We no longer fear the deadline creeping up on us. We instead continually work on getting there no matter how long it takes. That we tell ourselves we will get there no matter what, no matter how long. The key is to keep at it consistently and never give up.

Having the desire to work at an Apple store as a retail specialist, I never let myself say that I expect apple to hire me by a certain time otherwise I am never pursuing the job ever again. Rather I tell myself that being an Apple specialist is my dream job and that I will keep applying and trying and constantly trying to improve myself until Apple has no choice but to hire me one day. A deadline no longer bothers me anymore. While I wait for them to take me in, I will continue to pursue other areas of interest that will also move my life forward rather than letting circumstances dictate my actions. I know that I am always in control of my own ship and that I will get whatever I put my mind to eventually if I try hard enough.

So with that I challenge each and every one of you to be nicer to yourselves. Lower your lofty expectations and focus on the journey instead of the deadline. Learn to appreciate the little things around you and not let your ego get in the way.

I hope you learned something today, take care and I'll see you in the next one.

Chapter 13:

Stop Setting Unrealistic Expectations of Your Partner

Are you wondering how to stop unmet expectations from ruining your relationship? Do you find yourself constantly disappointed with your partner and thinking about ending it?

There are ways to stop unmet expectations from ruining your relationship. Here are a few.

1. Identify Your Own

One way to stop unmet expectations from ruining your relationship is by questioning your own. What do you think you need from your partner? Do you need him to give up his friends and hobbies for you? Do you expect to have sex every night? Do you want her to keep the house spotlessly clean as your mother did? Do you expect him to anticipate your every need?

Expectations like these are exactly the things that can kill a relationship. I would encourage you to think about what you want from your partner so that it's clear in your mind. I also want you to consider if your expectations are reasonable.

If your expectations aren't reasonable, your relationship might be dead upon arrival. If you don't know your expectations, your partner will have a hard time reaching them because you might always be moving the goal post. So, before unmet expectations destroy your relationship, make sure you know what yours are.

2. Set Boundaries

I always encourage new couples to set boundaries in their relationships as soon as possible To understand healthy relationship boundaries, look at the four walls of your house. Those walls are the structure that holds your life together. They hold your food and your bed and your possessions, and it's where you live your life.

Healthy boundaries are the same as those four walls of your house. They are the things that support your relationship as it matures. To have a healthy relationship that can grow and be fruitful, it must have structures and boundaries that support it. Healthy boundaries come in many shapes, sizes, and colors.

A few examples:

- Make sure you stay yourself
- Allow yourselves time apart
- Communication is important
- Mutual respect at all times

- Keep the power dynamic equal
- Making time for both sides of the family
- Respecting others friends and hobbies

Of course, each couple needs to decide what works for them, but every couple must establish some boundaries early and stick to them for the sake of their relationship.

3. Be Truthful

You must discuss this with your partner if your expectations aren't being met. One of the most common complaints that I hear from women is 'he should know what I need. I shouldn't have to tell him.' And this, I am afraid, is mostly impossible. Men would love to anticipate and meet our needs, but many of them just don't always have it in them. This is not some deficiency of character but because men have no idea how women think and why. It's a mystery to them, so expecting them to be able to do so will set you up for disaster.

Chapter 14:

How To Take Note of Your Flaws

We all have flaws. As much as we can try to pretend we are perfect, we will find out soon enough from life that we all have parts of us that fall short in one way or another.

This doesn't mean that we are inferior, rather that we have room for improvement. By reframing our flaws as areas of growth, we can change the way we see our weaknesses.

But before we can grow, we first need to identify exactly what areas in our lives that we actually need to work on. It is easy for many of us to go through our days without thinking too much about the important aspects that we are failing to address. And when the time comes for us to perform, we wonder why we always come up short.

We then berate ourselves and assume that we are no good or that we are worse than others. All because we were not acute and aware enough to work on our flaws consistently over a period of time.

If health is an issue for us, either because we feel we are not getting to our ideal weight or sugar level, or whatever it may be, we need to note the habits that are bringing us down and work to replace them with healthier ones that bring us good instead.

We do this, again, by the power of journaling. Only through journaling can we realize exactly how much we are eating, how many calories we are actually consuming each meal, and how can we replace or reduce our intake to reach our goals.

It is easy for us to assume each meal is independent of the other. But everything we consume adds up. A can of coke might not seem much in one sitting, but 3 cans over the course of the day can quickly add up.

By journaling each activity we are doing, writing down the aspects that we excelled at and ones where we fall short at, we can identify the exact mistakes that we are making in order to improve on them gradually each day.

As the saying goes, practice makes perfect. We don't expect to ace the test on the first try, so why should we expect our flaws to be corrected on the second if we do nothing to improve it?

Once we become painfully aware of every single action we are taking, we can then work backwards and deconstruct each activity To find the areas we can work on.

Trust me, Rome isn't built in a day, so taking note and taking action on your flaws is the only way you will see any long-term progress in anything that you do in life. Take care, I believe in you, and I'll see you in the next one.

Chapter 15:

Share Your Troubles Freely and Openly

Life is hard. We go through tons of challenges, problems, and obstacles every single day. We accumulate problems and stresses left right and Center. Absorbing each impact blow for blow.

Over time, these impacts will wear us down mentally and physically. Without a proper release channel, we find that our emotions spill over in ways when we least expect it. We get easily irritated, have a hard time falling asleep, have mood issues, and find ourselves even being temporarily depressed at times.

When we bottle negativity, it festers inside us without us realising what we have done. That is where releasing those tensions by pouring our heart and soul into friends, writing, journaling, and other outlets that allow us to express our feelings freely without judgement.

We may not all have friends that we can truly count on to share our deepest darkest secrets for fear that they might share these secrets unsuspectingly. If we do have these types of friends, treasure them and seek them out regularly to share your problems. By bouncing ideas off someone, we may even find a new solution to an old problem that we couldn't before. The other party may also be able to see things more objectively and with a unique perspective that is contrary to yours which you could potentially use to your advantage.

If writing things down is something that helps you cope with life, then by all means take a piece of paper and write down all the things that have been bothering you. Journal it, archive it. You may even write a song about it if that helps you process things better. Writing things down help us clear our minds and lets us see the big picture when we come back to it at a later date should we feel ready to address it. When things are too crazy, we may not have the mental capacity to handle everything being thrown at us at one go. So take the time to sort those feelings out.

You may also choose to just find a place that brings you relaxation. Whether it be going to the beach, or renting a hotel, or even just screaming at the top of your lungs. Let those feelings out. Don't keep it hidden inside.

IF all these things still don't work for you, you may want to try seeking help from a professional counsellor or therapist who can work out these issues you have in your life one by one. Never be afraid to book an appointment because your mental health is more important than the stigma associated with seeing a professional. You are not admitting you have a problem, you are simply acknowledge that there are areas in your life that you need assistance with. And that it is perfectly okay and perfectly normal to do so. Counsellors have the passion to serve, the passion to help, and that is why they chose that profession to being with. So seek their assistance and guidance as much as you need to.

Life isn't easy. But we can all take a conscious effort to regulate our emotions more healthily to live a long and balanced life.

Chapter 16:

Enjoying The Simple Things

Today we're going to talk about a topic that might sound cheesy, but trust me it's worth taking a closer look at. And that is how we should strive to enjoy the simple things in life.

Many of us think we need a jam packed schedule for the week, month, or year, to tell us that we are leading a very productive and purposeful life. We find ways to fill our time with a hundred different activities. Going to this event, that event, never slowing down. And we find ourselves maybe slightly burnt out by the end of it.

We forget that sometimes simplicity is better than complication. Have you sat down with your family for a simple lunch meal lately? You don't have to talk, you just have to be in each other's company and enjoying the food that is being served in front of you.

I found myself appreciating these moments more than I did running around to activities thinking that I needed something big to be worth my time. I found sitting next to my family on the couch watching my own shows while they watch theirs very rewarding. I found eating alone at my favourite restaurant while watching my favourite sitcom to be equally as enjoyable as hanging out with a group of 10 friends. I also found myself richly enjoying a long warm shower every morning and evening. It is the highlights of my day.

My point is that we need to start looking at the small things we can do each day that will bring us joy. Things that are within our control. Things that we know can hardly go wrong. This will provide some stability to gain some pleasure from. The little nuggets in the day that will not be determined by external factors such as the weather, friends bailing on us, or irritating customers.

When we focus on the little things, we make life that much better to live through.

Chapter 17:

Dealing with Abuse in Relationship

Why can't they simply leave the relationship? This is one question that people frequently ask when they see someone is being abused in a relationship. But if you are the one who is in an abusive relationship, you will know that it not this easy. Ending a relationship that means a lot to you is never easy to end. It gets even more difficult when you have been psychologically beaten down, physically threatened, isolated from your friends and family, and financially controlled. If you are in an abusive relationship and want to leave, you might be feeling torn or confused— one moment you want to leave, the other you want to stay. You might even blame yourself for the abuse. If you are in an abusive relationship, we want you to remember;

- You are not to blame for being battered or mistreated.

- You deserve a safe and happy life.

- You are not the cause of your partner's abusive behavior.

- You are not alone. People are waiting to help.

- You deserve to be treated with respect.

- Your children deserve a safe and happy life.

Now, when you have to decide whether to stay in a relationship or to leave, here are some of the things you should keep in mind:

If you're hoping abusive partners will change, that is probably not going to happen; these people have deep psychological and emotional issues; although change is not something that is impossible but is not easy or quick, and change is only possible if the abuser takes full responsibility for their behavior.

Suppose you believe you can help your abuser. In that case, that is a natural phenomenon you will that you are the only one who understands them or that it is your responsibility to fix their problems. Still, the actual truth is that when you stay, you accept constant abuse, and you enable them, so instead of helping them, you are perpetuating the problem.

Suppose your partner has promised to stop the abuse. In that case, that is probably what they say at the moment because when they face, the consequences they plead for another chance and promise to change or beg for forgiveness. They might even mean it at the moment, but their actual goal is to stay in control and keep you from leaving them, and as soon as you will forgive them, they will return to their abusive behavior as soon as you forgive them because they are no longer worried that you will leave them.

Even If your partner is in counseling, there is no guarantee that they will change; there are many abusers that go through and continue to be violent, aggressive, controlling, and abusive. Suppose your partner has stopped making excuses and is showing visible signs of change, then that is good. However, you should decide based on who they are right now, not on the hope of who they would become.

If you are worried about what will happen once you leave, it is valid to be afraid of your abusive partner's will and where you will go, or how you will support your children or yourself. But you should not let this fear of the unknown keep you in an abusive relationship.

Here are some signs that your abuser is not changing

- They minimize the abuse or denies how serious it was.
- They pressurize you to make decisions about the relationship.
- They say that they can't change unless you stay with him and support him.
- You have to push him to stay in treatment.
- They tell you that you owe him another chance.
- They try to get sympathy from you, your children, or your family and friends.
- They claim that you're the abusive one.
- They pressure you to go to couple's counseling.
- They expect something from you in exchange for getting help.
- They continue to blame others for his behavior.

Chapter 18:

10 Signs Your Ex Still Loves You

Breakups are very tough to handle. They shatter your heart and have you questioning all your life choices and decisions. You go through a lot of negative emotions, and these tend to be heightened because of the painful words, actions, broken promises, and broken bonds that you both once shared. Despite all of this, it's never easy to let go and move on from a once-strong relationship. There might still be some fragments left that'll give you the idea that maybe your ex is still not over you. Here are some signs you should see to know if your ex still loves you and wants you back.

1. **Following your online activities:**

If your ex still hasn't blocked you, instead follows all your updates on social media, it might show that they still have concern for you and would like to reconnect with you. The constant likes, comments, and reactions on your posts is also a way of showing that you're constantly on their mind, and they're still not ready to let you go.

2. Nostalgic conversations:

Suppose, by any chance, you converse with your ex, and they constantly try to reminisce about your happy moments together or mention how you both could have avoided ending things like this and should have dealt with issues better. In that case, that means they're regretting the breakup. This is also a way of testing how you would react to such conversations and see if another shot at this relationship is possible.

3. Reaching out from time to time:

Suppose your ex reaches out to you during special holidays and events, like your birthday or a wedding of a mutual or even christmas and halloween. In that case, it could be the perfect excuse for them to get closer to you without exposing much of their feelings. If they text you and ask for your help with something, no matter how small or stupid, they are just making efforts to be around you.

4. Staying a bit longer to talk:

You might be familiar with the feeling of joy that you experience each time you talk to a friend who seems close to you and with whom you love sharing things. No matter how much you've spoken or how late you're getting, you still hang with them for just a few minutes more. If you sense that your ex feels the same about you each time you guys meet or talk, they still have some feelings for you.

5. Showing signs of loneliness:

When your ex constantly seems gloomy and upset and lets the whole world know by posting it on social media, it could signify that they are seeking your attention. If they post sad stuff that's relatable to both of you, chances are they're waiting for you to notice it and reach out to them.

6. Trying to patch things up:

Your ex might finally hold themselves accountable for their actions and mistakes and often talk about what they should have done to save the relationship. They may constantly try to reassure you that they have changed and now they're a better person. If this is a recurring theme, then this is a vital sign they want you back.

7. Showing they miss you:

The most significant sign that your ex wants you back is most probably opening up to you and showing you how much they miss you. They might make you remember the old times and share stuff about how miserable they are without you. It's a clear sign that they still love you.

8. Available for help:

If your ex reaches out and offers you their assistance and is always available whenever you need help, they are still looking out for you.

This is a good indication showing that they will always be there for you no matter what, and you can rely on them.

9. Backed up by friends:

If your ex's friends or even your friends reach out to you and say that your ex has changed and they still talk about you a lot, they're making you consider going back with them. Chances are, your ex has made a good image in front of your circle to try and win you back.

10. Still single after a long time:

If a long time has passed since your breakup and your ex still hasn't opened up to the idea of dating, it means they still haven't moved on from you and are still lingering on the hope of getting back together with you.

Conclusion:

If you observe these signs with your ex, consider them carefully to make the right decision for yourself.

Chapter 19:

8 Signs You Need to Call it Quits

Intro:

Most of the times, we stretch our relationship to the point that it becomes unbearable for us to be with someone. We either fear uncertainty or be lonely that we push our boundaries of tolerance; the sole reason for doing that is to avoid pain. You need to take care of your happiness. The whole point of being with someone is to be happy. If there is no passion or romance left and your relationship feels stagnant, it is time for you to call it quits because from that point on, your relationship is only going to degrade, and you should leave before things take a turn for the worse. If you feel that you deserve better and have unmet emotional needs, there is no reason to continue the relationship. Even if you try your hardest, you can not twist the reality. If you are having trouble figuring out whether you should call it quits or not, we are going to give you 7 reasons why you should call it quits!

1. Lost Trust:

One of the essential parts of a relationship is "trust" it works like glue and holds a relationship together. Trust assures you that a person is loyal to you, and no matter what happens, they will always stay by your side.

The long-term survival of a relationship is not possible without trust. If you do not trust your partner, you will doubt their actions, and it will be bad for you and them because you will be acting like a detective checking upon them all the time, they will lose their freedom, and you will lose your peace of mind. If you do not trust your partner, you should just let them go.

2. You feel Unhappy:

All relationships feel amazing in the beginning. Later, you get to see their partner for who they are. The point of getting into a relationship is to feel happy and complete. If you feel anxious and full of pain, then what is the point of this relationship? You will start feeling lonely even when your partner is with you. If you feel sad and disappointed most of the time rather than happy and sad, it just means your partner does not think about you anymore. If you need to leave your partner to find peace, then it's time to call it quits.

3. Lack of Support:

It is essential to have a supportive and understanding partner if you want your relationship to grow. Your relationship becomes ten times harder if your partner does not believe in your dreams most of your time and energy will be consumed in convincing them that you are capable of doing that. If someone important in your life will continuously discourage you, negativity and self-doubt will surround you. Being with the wrong person will make you feel worthless all the time. If someone is hindering your growth and pulling you down, then you should cut them loose.

4. Zero Communication:

Lack of communication will lead to a lot of misunderstandings. If you do not sit with your partner to speak your mind with them, your emotions are bottled up and even when you do, they do not try to understand your perspective and instead play blame games this just results in hurting you more. If there is increased misunderstanding and you have tried to solve the issue multiple times, and the result is always the same, there is a high chance things are not going to change in the near future. There is a difference between not trying to communicate and not trying to understand the other person. If the case is later, then it's time to leave them for good.

5. Controlling Behavior:

It might be a bit difficult for you to identify between a caring partner and a controlling partner. But we are here to make things easy for you. A controlling partner always interferes in your business and will criticize you even for little things. The worst thing they will do is isolate you from your family and friends, and sometimes they will even try to turn them against you. They are insecure, so they will also ask you to not talk to certain people, mostly of the opposite gender. Plus, you will have to explain yourself a lot, and if you do not, it will lead to a fight.

6. Zero Efforts:

The key factor that leads to the growth of a relationship is an active effort from both sides. It is all in the efforts you make to get to know them, keep each other happy and take an interest in each other's life. A relationship does not survive if there is not enough effort from both sides. If there is a one-sided effort, then there will be a lot of burden on the person trying to make it work, and as a result, this will drain your energy and exhaust yourself. If your partner does not go beyond their comfort zone to be there for you will suffocate you.

7. Different Life Paths:

If you and your partner are on the same page, the relationship will go a long way. At first, you do not really care about the future because you are so engrossed in your relationship, but when you realize that this might affect your goals, it is difficult to carry on. You will think about it every day, and it will consume you, but you should remember no relationship is greater than your happiness.

Conclusion:

All of the relationships and people are different from each other some choose to leave a relationship for their dreams, and some might give up their dreams for love. What you need to do is find out what makes you happy and works for you. You need to set limits for yourself, and beyond those limits, you will not compromise or bend yourself. You should never forget the entire point of being in a relationship is to be happy, and so you can finally have someone who understands you. These are the two things you should never compromise on.

Chapter 20:

6 Ways To Deal With Rude People

Rudeness is not a quality everybody likes; on the contrary, most people tend to stay away from rude people, so they don't have to deal with them, but sometimes, we haven't got any options, avoiding them isn't an option. You can meet rude people in your work offices, schools, colleges, or any public place. You have to deal with them. When someone is disrespectful to us, all we want to do is snap back at them, but that would make you just like them. Here are a few ways to deal with rude people.

1. Try To Be Understanding

We have got those bad days when we don't want to talk to anyone and when someone talks to us, we respond a bit rudely even if we don't realize it. The person who's being rude to you could also be going through something right now. The best you can do is be understanding and give them some space. Eventually, they would realize and would apologize. If they don't apologize and continue being rude, just let it go; you can't change how someone wants to talk to people. Everybody has their habits. Even though being rude is not that good practice, it is still a habit, and to change a pattern, a person needs time and willpower.

2. Call Them Out On Their Behavior

As mentioned before, sometimes we don't realize when we ate being rude to someone, but that doesn't make us wrong. It is just that we are going through a particular phase in our life that causes us to be that way. So if someone is rude to you, call them out on their rudeness; if they care, they will indeed apologize. If they don't want to be sorry, then don't get upset, limit your contact with them, like talking to them only when necessary because it's difficult to completely stay away from that rude person if he is a co-worker or a neighbor.

3. Don't Backbite

Don't talk bad about that person behind his back to someone else. Firstly it would spread rumors, and people would not hesitate to gossip. Secondly, talking behind someone's back is also considered rude, so if you talk behind that person's back, what is the difference between you and that rude person. Thirdly, when you talk bad about someone, it will only cause the situation to get worse than it already is.

4. Avoid The Rude Person

Even when you call them out on your behavior but the person is still impolite towards you, don't stress; walk away. If they are rude, then it is their problem, not yours. You don't have you worry about it because there is nothing you can do. Just walk away and don't give that person the slightest chance to talk to you. Indeed, when everyone starts walking away from him, he would realize that this habit is not causing any good and would make an effort to change and become better.

5. Be More Kind

This way is more than complex, of course; who would want to be nice to someone who isn't nice to you, but when you offer some extra kindness, you will set an example for that person. Everybody loves a kind person. After a while of your service, the person would realize that you are kind and don't deserve his rudeness. The other person would eventually calm down and surely will follow your lead. It's hard to be rude to someone who is too kind towards you.

6. Rudeness Is Nothing New

Since the beginning of time, rudeness has been a part of human nature; there is nothing new. No matter what you do, you will always find rude people everywhere you go. All you need to do is accept that this is nothing new and you can't change the way these people think, maybe it is their habit, and perhaps they will change this with time, but there is nothing you can do about it, so don't fret.

Conclusion

Don't take the words of rude people to heart. The world is full of rudeness; no matter what you do, you can't get rid of them. But there is one thing you can do, be the kind and loving person that you are. Don't be rude to them, just be kind towards them. Indeed with time, everybody realizes their bad habits. And don't worry about it, at least you are not among the rude people.

Chapter 21:

8 Tips On Meeting Your Partner's Family

Although first impressions aren't always an accurate representation of who we are, we can't deny that they leave some impact. They're a way for people to create an idea of how we are and who they deem us to be. Meeting your partner's family for the very first time can be stressful. It would be best if you didn't look unprepared, nor look overly prepared. While you might be tense about messing things up, here are some tricks and tips to ensure that your meeting with your partner's family goes pleasant.

1. **Learn the family dynamic beforehand:**

Start by gaining insight into your partner's family by asking them questions about their family members, that is, ask your partner if their dad has an authoritarian personality? Are they a family of values and rules or just casually jokes around with each other? The key isn't knowing the scenario that's coming but preparing yourself for one that could form. You don't have to change yourself or your personality to fit in, and you just have to be a bit careful and gather your thoughts before meeting them.

2. Prepare for small talk:

Put down that list of topics you've been preparing for a month and take a deep breath. While it's good to rehearse the curated summary of the questions they might ask you, it's even better if you will let the conversation flow naturally. You will feel less pressured and more at ease with having open-ended questions at hand.

3. Be mindful of your attire:

Yes, you do look sexy in that black mini skirt of yours, and you do consider this ensemble a classic, but there's a time and place for dresses like these. Try picking out sophisticated outfits, not scandalous ones. After all, you have to avoid all the unnecessary judgments on your first meeting. Play it safe and choose one that you might look your best in and one that would be approved by both your partner and their family.

4. Attempt to help out:

If you're meeting them at their house for either lunch, tea, or dinner, make sure to offer your help to them. As much as your ability to converse won't go unnoticed, your gesture to help out is the one thing that will get you brownie points. Ask them if you could pile up the dishes for them or help them set the table. However, if they consistently say no, then back off. Don't continue insisting.

5. Respect the family rules:

The moment you step inside their house and under their roof, you're bound to follow their rules and values. Keeping knowledge of the family rules is just as crucial as your willingness to respect them. Maybe your partner's family would want you to take off your shoes and wear house slippers or would like you to pray with them before eating. Nonetheless, rules are rules, and you have to respect and follow them, even if you disagree with some of them.

6. Bring a gift:

Gifts are always a symbol of affection and consideration. Decide on a thoughtful gift and put in a little extra effort. You will start on a good foot with their family and could continue this positive impression as the night goes on. You can ask your partner about some ideas too.

7. Put your phone away:

While you won't be stupid enough to be on your phone with them, it's important to get reminded again. You might start scrolling your newsfeed in nervousness, or your habit of refreshing your timeline may get the best of you, but it's crucial to avoid such behavior in front of your partner's family. Tune out all the other disturbances and keep your focus on the conversations you're having with them.

8. Relax:

Even though you might feel your soul leave your body, try to breathe and relax. Take pride in who you are and be confident in yourself. Of course, don't ruin things by being too overconfident. Get a pep talk with yourself or your partner and comfort yourself. The right people will recognize and accept and appreciate you just as you are.

Conclusion:

Test the waters as you go. Don't go all in at the first second, but instead, come out of your shell slowly and steadily. Be polite, thoughtful, and smile; you've got this and can't go wrong!

Chapter 22:

Saying Yes To Things

Today we're going to talk about why saying yes can be a great thing for you and why you should do so especially in social invites.

Life you see is a funny thing. As humans, we tend to see things one dimensionally. And we tend to think that we have a long life ahead of us. We tend to take things for granted. We think we will have time to really have fun and relax after we have retired and so we should spend all our efforts and energy into building a career right now, prioritising it above all else. When faced with a choice between work and play, sometimes many of us, including myself choose work over social invites.

There were periods in my life that i routinely chose work over events that it became such a habit to say no. Especially as an entrepreneur, the interaction between colleagues or being in social events is almost reduced to zero. It became very easy and comfortable to live in this bubble where my one and only priority in life is to work work work. 24 hours, 7 days a week. Of course, in reality a lot of time was wasted on social media and Netflix, but u know, at least i could sort of pretend that i was kind of working all day. And I was sort of being productive and sort of working towards my goals rather than "wasting time on social events". That was what I told myself anyway.

But life does not work that way. As I prioritised work over all else, soon all the social invite offers started drying up. My constant "nos" were becoming evident to my social circle and I was being listed as perpetually unavailable or uninterested in vesting time or energy into any friendships or relationships. And as i retreated deeper and deeper into this black hole of "working remotely" i found myself completely isolated from new experiences and meeting new people, or even completely stopped being involved in any of my friend's lives.

I've successfully written myself out of life and I found myself all alone in it.

Instead of investing time into any meaningful relationships, I found that my closest friends were my laptop, tablet, phone, and television. Technology became my primary way of interacting with the world. And I felt connected, yet empty. I was always plugged in to wifi, but i lived my life through a screen instead of my own two eyes. My work and bedroom became a shell of a home that I spent almost all my time, and life just became sort of pointless. And I just felt very alone.

As I started to feel more and more like something was missing, I couldn't quite make out what it was that led me to this feeling. I simply though to myself, hey I'm prioritising work and my career, making money is what the internet tells me I should do, and not having a life is simply part of the price you have to pay... so why am I so incredibly unhappy?

As it turns out, as I hope many of you have already figured out at this point, that life isn't really just about becoming successful financially.

While buying a house, getting a car, and all that good stuff is definitely something that we should strive towards, we should not do so at the expense of our friends. That instead of saying no to them, we should start saying yes, at least once in a while. We need to signal to our friends that hey, yes even though I'm very busy, but I will make an effort to carve out time for you, so that you know I still value you in my life and that you are still a priority.

We need to show our friends that while Monday may not work for us, that I have an opening maybe 2 weeks later if you're still down. That we are still available to grow this friendship.

I came to a point in my life where I knew something had to change. As I started examining my life and the decisions I had made along the way with regards to my career, I knew that what I did wrong was saying no WAAAAAY too often. As I tried to recall when was the last time I actually when I went out with someone other than my one and only BFF, I simply could not. Of the years that went by, I had either said that I was too busy, or even on the off chances that I actually agreed to some sort of meetup, I had the habit of bailing last minute on lunch and dinner appointments with friends. And I never realized that i had such a terrible reputation of being a flaker until I started doing some serious accounting of my life. I had become someone that I absolutely detested without even realising it. I have had people bail on me at the very last minute before, and I hated that feeling. And whenever someone did that to me, I generally found it difficult to ask them out again because I felt that they weren't really that interested in meeting me anyway. That they didn't even bother to reschedule the appointment. And little did I know, I was becoming that very same person and doing the very thing that I hate to my friends. It is no wonder that I started dropping friends like flies with my terrible actions.

As I came to this revelation, I started panicking. It was as if a truck had hit me so hard that I felt that I was in a terrible accident. That how did I let myself get banged up to that extent?

I started scrolling through my contact lists, trying to find friends that might still want to hang out with me. I realized that my WhatsApp was basically dry as a desert, and my calendar was just work for the last 3 years straight with no meaningful highlights, no social events worth noting.

It was at this point that I knew I had made a huge mistake and I needed to change course immediately. Salvaging friendships and prioritising social activities went to the top of my list.

I started creating a list of friends that I had remotely any connection to in the last 5 years and I started asking them out one by one. Some of my friends who i had asked out may not know this, but at that point in my life, i felt pretty desperate and alone and I hung on to every meeting as if my life depended on it. Whilst I did manage to make some appointments and met up with some of them. I soon realized that the damage had been done. That my friends had clearly moved on without me... they had formed their own friends at work and elsewhere, and I was not at all that important to have anymore. It was too little too late at that point and there was not much I could do about it. While I made multiple attempts to ask people out, I did not receive the same offers from people. It felt clearly like a one-way street and I felt that those people that I used to call friends, didn't really see me as one. You see growing a friendship takes time, sometimes years of consistent meetups before this person becomes indispensable in your life. Sharing unique experiences that allow your friends to see that you are truly vested in them and that you care about them and want to spend time with them. I simply did not give myself that chance to be integrated into someone's life in that same way, I did not invest that time to growing those friendships and I paid the price for it.

But I had to learn all these the hard way first before I can receive all the good that was about to come in the future.

In the next piece, I will show how i actually turned my life around by putting myself in positions where I will be exposed to more chances of social activity. And when saying yes became critical to growing a new social network for myself.

Chapter 23:

9 Ways Women Fall In Love

Opening

What makes a woman fall in love with men? Different TV shows and movies portray various scenarios of women falling in love only with rich and handsome guys. Think the Bachelor or some cheesy dating show. As a result we are incline to think that women will only like us if we are rich and handsome as well. But in reality women are far more complex and do see past the money, glamour, and attractive looks, to something that holds more dearly to their heart.

While women fall in love differently than men, they strongly desire their partners to respect, understand, love, and appreciate them for who they are. As a guy, it can be complicated to know the different ways that women fall in love with men. We make this easier for you. In this video, we will share eight different ways that they do just that. Let's get started!

1. She desires to be familiar with you

While this is true for both sexes, women show a greater desire to know their partner through spending quality time and making meaningful memories together. This helps them develop a more profound understanding of a potential soul mate. A woman wants to know if he is the one that she can build a memorable future together. On the contrary, men tend to favor the need to feel attraction in the beginning of a relationship, which I must say is usually mostly physical.

If she desires to be familiar with you, it is a sign that she might be considering you for the part. It is significant to remember that while physical looks are important, your personality and a deep personal and emotional connection is the one that will determine if a woman will fall in love with you.

2. They look for thoughtfulness

Being highly thoughtful themselves, women feel excited and much happier with a thoughtful man. They fancy feeling special, desired, and appreciated a top priority in an ideal partner that can give that to them. Receiving a sweet text message or flowers is extremely romantic for many women. They also truly admire men who remember special dates and occasions. If you can do these things with your eyes closed, you have already won half the battle.

3. She wants to know your Thoughts

Estrogen is known as the female sex hormone and it plays an integral role in remembering special memoirs, comprehending abstract conceptions, and other general webbed thoughts. A woman wants to know that her partner can initiate and understand meaningful or logical perceptions.

While it is wonderful to connect with someone through enjoyable dates and activities, women don't fall in love unless they are attracted to someone's thought-oriented personality. Do we appreciate similar life perspectives? Does he inspire me to advance my life knowledge? Intelligence is the most important aspect of a healthy relationship. A woman does not look for an intelligent partner to answer her questions, but she is particularly interested in discovering momentous life philosophies with her partner.

4. She desires to have a great communicator

Being able to have regular great conversations with a man is something highly sought after in women. Women often fall in love knowing they can engage in healthy communications with their partners. Having a meaningful connection is key here.

Do you know women particularly check the verbal communication skills of their partners to establish a deeper understanding of their personalities? It does not mean women don't appreciate silence, but a good balance between the two is the takeaway here. Women fall in love with guys who participate in good debates that challenge them intellectually without coming across as arrogant.

5. Value for Family

It's highly attractive for women to see a man giving higher consideration to his or her family. A woman truly appreciates a man who takes great care of his family and treats them with due respect. It is an obvious sign that he will give the same amount of respect to her as well. She feels truly grateful when he introduces her to his parents and exerts all his efforts to win the hearts of her family.

While we may not be able to control how family members think and behave, it is the effort and initiative of a man to win their approval that makes them the apple of any woman's eye.

6. She wants to have a trustworthy partner

While it may be controversial to say in this day and age, biologically, women are child-bearers. If having a child is a priority for a woman, they will naturally have a desire to find someone who is proven to be a reliable and trustworthy partner. A partner that will prioritize being a father some day and all that major responsibilities that come with it as a result. A woman will fall in love with a man knowing that they will be able to provide and take care of the family in the future.

If having kids is not a priority, having a trustworthy partner in other areas such as fidelity is also significant for a woman. Knowing she can trust you will be an easy way to win over her heart.

7. She desires to know if she can be herself with you

While it equally applies to both men and women, it does not lessen its significance when a woman determines it before falling in love. Since vulnerability is a widely accepted element in having sincere feelings for someone, a woman wishes to know if you can accept her for who she is without changing anything about her. A woman truly falls for a guy who accepts her the way she is and appreciates her presence in his life.

8. Please be gentle, man

Now last but not least...!

A woman will never give her sincere feelings to someone who is not gentle to her. Having a supportive, loving, caring, and easygoing partner is one of the top elements that women consider while falling in love.

Having a trustworthy and gentle partner to navigate through life's journey is the fundamental priority of every woman.

Thank you!

Chapter 24:

8 Signs You Were Actually In Love

Falling in love is something some of us might have experienced, but others? They might be new to this feeling, and they might not even know its love. There is no way someone could tell you are in love except for you. Unlike disney princesses, a bird isn't going to come flying and whisper it in your ear. You have to check the facts and feelings in this case. Initially, love will feel very exciting and adventurous, but eventually, you will be settled and calm. Love is a colorful feeling. And here are some ways you can make sure that what you feel towards someone is love.

1. You feel thrilled around them:

When the person you like excites you and makes you feel ecstatic. Then you got it. You are in love with them. But don't be so sure right away; it can be affected by adrenaline rushes in your body. But mostly, it's the feeling of butterflies fluttering in your stomach and doing somersaults. Your excitement is not expected but above average.

2. You want to see them again and again:

Even if they have just left, you always wait to see them again. You wait for the hours where you will see them. If you, by any reason, have to see them daily, then except for getting boring, it gets exciting and interesting day by day. Even though it's not healthy to not let them leave, you must calm down. It is common in love.

3. You always smile around them:

It's hard to stay severe and uptight when someone you love is around. So, whenever they make a conversation with you, you always smile. You visit happily around them, and that makes your mood go up a thousand folds. When you enjoy being around someone, it's natural. Just make sure to keep that jaw in check.

4. You see the good in them:

When we fall in love with someone, all we see is the good in them. Their sound quality becomes the highlight of their personality, and their flaws seem small and irrelevant. You ignore their bad habits because of one good quality they might have because, in love, flaws don't matter. The good always attracts people, and that is what might have tempted you towards them and forward with love with them.

5. Imagining a future with them:

We can't imagine a future with anyone we see and get attracted to. But when you start to imagine a lot with someone, it's apparent that you want to spend it with them. You might want to make them a part of your real life. And it can also happen with a bit of effort and communication. It will work out in the end.

6. You change yourself a little:

Shaping yourself according to someone's need sure sounds unhealthy, but it's a true sign of love. When you do things that they might like and make yourself acknowledged by them, then you want their attention all to yourself. You dress nicely, you put on makeup, and talk more confidently. These are all the basics you do to impress them with your charm and your will to make them fall in love with you.

7. You are overprotected by them:

You have a hawk-like gaze on everyone that watches over your love interest. Especially your same gender. Possessiveness is fine until it becomes extreme. You know all the people who talk to them and ensure that some particular stay away from them. We all understand this level of love, and it is okay to be overprotective of your loved one.

8. You change your priorities:

When you change your sense of style and mindset, it's evident that next in the line is the priority. They come a level higher every time they do the minimum for you. And eventually, you won't even notice, and they are much higher on that list to ignore. That is why keeping them a priority changes many aspects of your life, making you happy for the good.

Conclusion:

Falling in love is harmless and colorful. It's exciting and wholesome. All the words might not be enough to describe it, but it's a good feeling. You have to accept that you are in love with a person and need to do something about it. You need to let them know and believe your feelings, and you never know? They might feel the same.

Chapter 25:

6 Tips To Have A Healthy Long Distance Relationship

Who says long-distance relationships don't last? Well, a lot of your friends and family members would be against it, they would discourage it, and will advise you not to take it too seriously as for them, it'll only lead to your heartbreak. Honestly, it's not going to be easy. Long-distance would make most of the things unachievable, it could get complicated at times, and you will find yourself vulnerable, sad, and lonely. However, that extra distance also plays a role in getting both of you closer. Studies have found that long-distance relationships don't differ significantly from geographically close relationships, and even in some cases, it might even be better.

First of all, you should be comforted in knowing that long-distance relationships can succeed. With that in mind, we have combined a list of tips that will keep your long-distance relationship healthy and ensure that it lasts.

Technology Is Your Best Friend

In this age of facetime-ing and texting without paying sky-high rates, long-distance relationships are now easier than ever. You can share the day-to-day minutia with your partner by instantaneously sharing photos, exchanging texts and calls, and skyping one another. It'sIt's much different than writing a letter to your loved one and waiting weeks or months for a response. People in long-distance relationships also rely more heavily on technology to stay connected with each other. This helps them communicate verbally even more than the couples who see each other often, sit in the same room, and do not interact at all. It's essential not just to generalize but to share details with your partner. It would make both of you feel like you've witnessed each other's day.

Be Commited to The Relationship

This implies to everyone involved in relationships, but especially to people who are pursuing long-distance relationships. It's crucial to know that you're committed to only one person and that you love them before wasting your time as well as theirs. If you're choosing to stay in a long-distance relationship, you both must sort out where you both stand in life, what will happen next in your relationship, and that you both work towards a goal. It can be daunting to plan your future around another person, but it can do wonders for you both if we both work it through. Be vocal about your feelings so that the other person doesn't live in darkness about what you want.

Set An End Date

While long-distance love can be magical, but it's only a great thing for a finite time. Eventually, you would crave wanting to be in the same place as your partner. It can be hard to stay apart for a long time. One thing that'll help couples in this drastic time is to schedule a meeting and look forward to it every day. Both must stay equally committed to the relationship and should be on the same page about how long this situation would last. You and your partner's plans should align in eventually living in the same place.

Do Stuff Together, Even Though You're Apart

If you aren't physically in the same place, it doesn't mean you both can't have fun together. You can plan a movie night via skype or cook something together while facetime-ing each other. There are loads of streaming services available that make it easier to binge-watch your favorite shows with your partner. Apart from that, you can also search for some quizzes or games online that will connect both of you and help you find more about each other. You can also raise controversial topics and spark new and exciting conversations to see your partner's stance.

Make Fun Plans For When You Both Will Meet

Indulge into details of what the two of you will do the next time you see each other. Make it a ritual of discussing all of the stuff with your partner that you so eagerly look forward to doing with them. Be it trying new restaurants every day, or picking up a holiday destination, or simply choosing a new hobby to do together. You can also schedule good night video calls in your PJs to create a sense of you going to bed together.

Set Clear Rules and Boundaries

Don'tDon't do anything that you wouldn't expect your partner to do either. Try your best to stay out of situations that might make your partner feel insecure or uncomfortable. You don't have to check in with your partner for every approval, but you should set clear boundaries for the both of you and adhere to them.

Conclusion

It can get lonely and difficult sometimes when dealing with long-distance but know that the fruits, in the end, will be as sweet as heaven. Constantly inject positive energy into your relationship to keep it alive. Be grateful for your partner and be thankful for the fact that there's someone who loves you and whom you love.

Chapter 26:

6 Signs You May Be Lonely

What is that one emotion that leads us to anxiety, depression, or stress? People often feel this emotion when they have no one around to support them. That is being lonely. What is being lonely? "When one is unable to find life's meaning," or simply put, it is the feeling of isolation. You often find yourself in a corner then outside with friends or family. Sometimes, these emotions are triggered by discouragement by close ones and negativity of life. We try to bear it alone rather than risking the judgment of others. We try to hide it as much as possible. Then, eventually, it becomes a habit. Then even if it's news worth sharing, we keep it to ourselves.

Loneliness can drive a person to harm themselves, either physically or mentally, or both too. It can change our lives drastically. Going out seems to be a burden. It feels tiresome even to move an inch. So, we tend to stay in one place, probably alone. But it doesn't always mean that you are feeling sad. Sometimes you feel happy being alone. It all depends on how you look at things.

1. Feeling Insecure

When we look around us, we see people every day. This type of connection with people can lead to two conclusions. Positive or negative.

A positive attitude may lead to appreciation. However, negative emotions will lead to insecurities. This insecurity will lead us to go out as little as possible. And whatever we hate about us, we feel it more prominent. Eventually, we never go out at all. Because of the fear that people might judge us at our worst trait. We think that even our family is against us, which makes it even more difficult.

2. Anger Becomes A Comrade

It becomes hard to express what we feel to others. When we feel like there is no one we can genuinely tell our feeling to, they bottle up. We start to bottle up our emotions to don't get a chance to tell others about them. And those bottle-up emotions turn into anger the most easily. Even the slightest thing could make us aggressive. We get angry over all petty stuff, and gradually, it becomes our release to all the emotion. It becomes easier to show your anger than other emotions.

3. It Starts To Hurt Us Physically

Stress is one of the feelings you get out of being lonely. It is only natural that you stress about everything when you are alone in a situation. Scientifically, it is proven that staying alone most of the time raises our stress hormone, and it becomes a heart problem in the future. Most of us have experienced the tightening of our chest at times. That is when our stress hormone raises it builds up around our heart. It may also result in inflammation and some vascular problems. So, being lonely all the time may be physically harmful to us, and we should take it seriously.

4. Highly Harmful To Mental Health

Mental health is just as important as physical health. We need to focus on both equally. Loneliness can be harmful to our mental health in many ways. It often leads to hallucinations. It causes depression and anxiety. These types of mental occurrences are proven fatal if not dealt with immediately. It also drives us to overthink, which is equally as harmful as others. Isolation keeps your brain in a constant phase of resentment.

5. Lack Of Hope and Self-Compassion

Getting lonely sometimes is okay. It gets serious when you do not want to let go of it. When there is no hope, it feels like there is no reason to return—staying alone forces you into feeling empty and unwanted, thus, losing hope of ever being wanted again. Because discouragement surrounds us, we feel safe staying alone most of the time. We lose all the passion we once had, and it makes us dull. Things that once we loved doing feel like a burden. Gradually, we become addicted.

6. Negativity

Positivity and negativity are two aspects of daily life. And in life, when loneliness is our companion, we choose negativity to go through our day. Everything seems to be too much work, and everything in life seems dark. Negativity is the only thing we keep because it looks more suitable to lonely people. It causes emotional harm to people and tends to get in the way of an average daily routine. However, the negative side is what we choose every day.

Conclusion

We can feel lonely even after being surrounded by people because it's just something people feel in themselves. They don't realize that there are people who are willing to talk to them. Being lonely can cause one a lot of harm and disrupt all the day's work. But it doesn't always mean that lonely people are unhappy. Loneliness can bring peace too.

Chapter 27:

6 Lessons You Can Learn From A Breakup

Have you ever been in a relationship, and it hasn't ended well? Breakups may make you feel insecure about yourself; if your significant other has broken up with you, you might feel rejected. Although watching tv shows and eating a tub of ice cream may sound like the only logical thing to do after a breakup, it is the time to focus on yourself and see what went wrong in your previous relationship. Relationships teach us who exactly we are, it tells us what kind of people we want to love. Here are a few lessons you can learn from a breakup.

1. Happiness Comes From Within

At the start of a relationship, we all feel excited and beyond happy, but happiness is not true happiness. Happiness comes from within. This means that we don't want to have anyone else in our life to feel happy. Sure, you would feel lonely after a breakup, but time heals everything. When you are with someone who doesn't treat you the way you should be treated, then you might've forgotten your self-worth. You need to remember that you were not born with this person; this relationship was just a part of your life. You need to start loving yourself, start accepting that this is the way you are. Once you start believing that only you can make yourself truly happy, you will finally understand the true meaning of happiness.

2. It's About Us

Breakup helps you to understand that it was never about them; it was always about you. When going through a breakup, people often blame everything on their significant other, but it is not always about them. Breakup gives you space for your personal growth. A breakup is very enlightening, although it may bring out some insecurities but as soon as you tackle your inner demons, you realize that it is all about you.

3. You Can't Change Anyone

Haven't we all heard someone saying that we will change them? It may sound effortless trying to change someone's habits, but it is pretty impossible in reality. We cannot change someone unless that person also wants to change. Change comes from within, and not even your love can change your partner. If you and your partner broke up, it probably was for the best even though opposites attract, but too many differences can cause many problems. It is time to accept the fact that you need to find someone who satisfies your needs.

4. Believe In Your Gut

When something isn't right or the way it should be, we all feel about it; it can be our instincts warning us. Listen to your gut. Often, we tend to ignore what our gut is telling us, and we carry on like everything is fine when it is the opposite. Sometimes, your gut tells you that this is not the one, but ignoring it will lead to a bad breakup. So always listen to what your gut has to say; it's just your heart telling you what it wants.

5. Figure Out What Your Heart Truly Wants

When we go through a breakup, we all know it happened for a reason; there was something about that relationship that you didn't want. Now is the time to figure out what you want from a relationship. It is the time to focus on yourself, understand your emotional needs, and how you want a relationship to be. It is time to figure out what kind of a relationship you want. Once you figure this out, you know what you do and what you don't want from a relationship.

6. It Is Okay To Be Alone

After a breakup, some people feel abandoned as if they are all alone now, and they feel like it is not a good thing, but in reality, it is okay to be alone; you don't always need to be with someone. When you realize that you can make yourself happy and you don't want anyone else to do that, it is the time when you need to become selfish and think about yourself. Set some goals, achieve them, and don't just throw yourself into another relationship without figuring out what you truly want because it may just end up in heartbreak.

Conclusion

Breakups are hard to go through, but they happen for a reason; try to figure out what indeed went wrong. What you want from a relationship and remember it is okay to be alone; you don't need someone else to make you feel happy. You are enough for yourself.

Chapter 28:

6 Behaviours That Keep You Single

Dating may not be as easy as it is shown in all those romantic Hollywood movies. There is so much more than appearance and stability in dating someone. And when you are old enough to be involved with someone, you sometimes find yourself uninterested. You think about how everyone your age has already started dating while you are back there eating junk and watching Netflix. It might appear to you that being in a relationship is tiresome, and you stop trying for it. Everyone has a different preference when it comes to finding someone for themselves. You tend to look for someone that matches your knight in the shining armor, which makes it hard for you to find someone you need.

Be true to you yourself while finding someone to date. Looking for someone with the expectation that you are rich and handsome would be foolish. It would be best if you worked on yourself more than that. Make yourself ease around with people but no so much that they start to get annoyed. Don't get in your way.

1. **Trust Is Essential**

Trusting each other is an important factor for dating someone. If you don't trust your partner even in the slightest, then nothing will matter. You will constantly doubt each other. Both of you will eventually fall apart if there is no trust. And if you have trust issues, it will be difficult for you to find someone worthy. But, if you trust too quickly, then it's only natural that you will break your bubble of expectations. Be friendly. Try to get to know them properly before making any assumptions about them. You don't want to go around hesitating about everything. Find yourself a reliable partner that trusts you too.

2. Too Many Expectations

Expecting too much from your partner will lead to only one thing. It leads towards Disappointment. It would help if you let them be. Don't expect things to go your way always. Your knight in the shining armor may be a bookworm because people find love in the most unexpected places. It doesn't always mean to keep no expectations at all. To keep the expectations low. You will get surprised constantly when you don't know what's coming your way. Don't let people cloud your judgment, and keep high standards about a relationship. Everyone has their share of ups and downs. Comparison with others will not be suitable for your relationship.

3. Have Self-Confidence

One has to respect itself before anything else can. You have to have self-esteem in you for people to take you seriously. It is true "you can't love someone unless you learn to love yourself first." You tend to feel insecure about yourself. Everything around you seems too perfect for you. And you constantly think that your partner will stop loving you one day. That fear of yours will get you nowhere. Try to give yourself as much care you can. It doesn't hurt to be loved.

4. Don't Overthink

You found a guy, and He seems to be excellent. But you start to overthink it. Eventually, you let go. That is what you shouldn't have done. Just try to go with the flow sometimes. Don't try too hard for it. Go for it the easy way. Overthinking will lead you to make up scenarios that never happened. Just let it be and see where it goes. Be easy so people can approach you. Think, don't overthink.

5. Involving Too Many People

When you initially start dating, you get nervous. People get help from their friends sometimes. But it is not necessary to get every move through them. Involving them in everything will only get your partner get uncomfortable and get you frustrated. People tend to give a lot of opinions of their own. You will get confused. So, it is good to keep these things to yourself. Be mindful in giving them a brief report from time to time. However, keep them at a reasonable distance.

6. Giving Up Too Quickly

If it doesn't work initially, it does not mean that it will never work. Patience is an essential element when it comes to dating anyone. Don't give up too quickly. Try to make it work until it's clear that it won't. Give it your all. Compromise on things you can. Because if both of you are not willing to compromise, it will not work between you both. It will work out in the end if it's meant to be. Don't push it if it's not working too.

Conclusion

It is hard; it keeps going at a pace. But all you must need is that spark that keeps it alive. Make it work until it doesn't. Go for it all. Make commitments only when you are sure about your choice. And be true to your words. Who wants to be single forever?

Chapter 29:

6 Signs You Are Emotionally Unavailable

In times of need, all we want is emotional comfort. The people around us mainly provide it. But the question is, will we support them if the need arises? You might be emotionally unavailable for them when they need you. It is necessary to have some emotional stability to form some strong bonds. If you are emotionally unapproachable, you will have fewer friends than someone you stand mentally tall. It is not harmful to be emotionally unavailable, but you need to change that in the long run. And for that, you need to reflect on yourself first.

It would help if you always were your top priority. While knowing why you are emotionally unapproachable, you need to focus on yourself calmly. Giving respect and talking is not enough for someone to rely on you. You need to support them whenever needed. Talk your mind with them. Be honest with them. But not in a rude way, in a comforting way. So, next time they will come to you for emotional support and comfort. If you are relating to all these things, then here are some signs that confirm it.

1. You Keep People At A Distance

It is usual for an emotionally unavailable person to be seen alone at times. They tend to stay aloof at times; that way, they don't have to be emotionally available. And even if you meet people, you always find it challenging to make a bond with them. You might have a few friends and family members close to you. But you always find meeting new people an emotionally draining activity. You also might like to hang out with people, but opening up is not your forte. If you are emotionally unavailable, then you keep people at a hands distance from you.

2. You Have Insecurities

If you struggle to love yourself, then count it as a sign of emotional stress. People are likely to be unavailable emotionally for others when they are emotionally unavailable for themselves too. We always doubt the people who love us. How can they when I, myself, can't? And this self-hatred eventually results in a distant relationship with your fellow beings. Pampering yourself time by time is essential for every single one of us. It teaches us how one should be taken care of and how to support each other.

3. You Have A Terrible Past Experience

This could be one of the reasons for your unapproachable nature towards people. When you keep some terrible memory or trauma stored inside of you, it's most likely you cannot comfort some other being. It won't seem like something you would do. Because you keep this emotional difference, you become distant and are forced to live with those memories, making things worse. It would help if you talked things out. Either your parents or your friends. Tell them whatever is on your mind, and you will feel light at heart. Nothing can change the past once it's gone, but we can work on the future.

4. You Got Heartbroken

In most cases, people are not born with this nature to be emotionally unavailable. It often comes with heartbreak. If you had a breakup with your partner, that could affect your emotional life significantly. And if it was a long-term relationship, then you got emotionally deprived. But on the plus side, you got single again. Ready to choose from scratch. Instead, you look towards all the negative points of this breakup. Who knows, maybe you'll find someone better.

5. You Are An Introvert

Do you hate going to parties or gatherings? Does meeting with friends sound tiresome? If yes, then surprise, you are an introvert. Social life can be a mess sometimes. Sometimes we prefer a book to a person. That trait of ours makes us emotionally unavailable for others. It is not a bad thing to stay at home on a Friday night, but going out once in a while may be healthy for you. And the easiest way to do that is to make an extrovert friend. Then you won't need to make an effort. Everything will go smoothly.

6. You Hate Asking For Help

Do you feel so independent that you hate asking for help from others? Sometimes when we get support from others, we feel like they did a favor for us. So, instead of asking for help, we prefer to do everything alone, by ourselves. Asking for aid, from superior or inferior, is no big deal. Everyone needs help sometimes.

Conclusion

Being emotionally unavailable doesn't make you a wrong person, but being there for others gives us self-comfort too. It's not all bad to interact with others; instead, it's pretty fun if you try. It will make your life much easier, and you will have a lot of support too.

Chapter 30:

6 Signs You Have A Fear of

Intimacy

Intimacy avoidance or avoidance anxiety, also sometimes referred to as the fear of intimacy, is characterized as the fear of sharing a close emotional or physical relationship with someone. People who experience it do not consciously want to avoid intimacy; they even long for closeness, but they frequently push others away and may even sabotage relationships for many reasons.

The fear of intimacy is separate from the fear of vulnerability, though both of them can be closely intertwined. A person who has a fear of intimacy may be comfortable becoming vulnerable and showing their true self to their trusted friends and relatives. This problem often begins when a person finds relationships becoming too close or intimate. Fear of intimacy can stem from several causes. Overcoming this fear and anxiety can take time, but you can work on it if you know the signs of why you have the fear in the first place.

1. Fear Of Commitment

A person who has a fear of intimacy can interact well with others initially. It's when the relationship and its value grow closer that everything starts to fall apart. Instead of connecting with your partner on an intimate level, you find ways and excuses to end the relationship and replace it with yet another superficial relationship. Some might even call you a 'serial dater,' as you tend to lose interest after a few dates and abruptly end the relationship. The pattern of emerging short-term relationships and having a 'commitment phobia' can signify that you fear intimacy.

2. Perfectionism

The idea of erfectionism often works to push others away rather than draw them near. The underlying fear of intimacy often lies in a person who thinks he does not deserve to be loved and supported. The constant need for someone to prove themself to be perfect and lovable can cause people to drift apart from them. Absolute perfectionism lies in being imperfect. We should be able to accept the flaws of others and should expect them to do the same for us. There's no beauty in trying to be perfect when we know we cannot achieve it.

3. Difficulty Expressing Needs

A person who has a fear of intimacy may have significant difficulty in expressing needs and wishes. This may stem from feeling undeserving of another's support. You need to understand that people cannot simply 'mind read,' they cannot know your needs by just looking at you; this might cause you to think that your needs go unfulfilled and your feelings of unworthiness are confirmed. This can lead to a vicious cycle of you not being vocal about your needs and lacking trust in your partner, and your relationship is meant to doom sooner or later.

4. Sabotaging Relationships

People who have a fear of intimacy may sabotage their relationship in many ways. You might get insecure, act suspicious, and accuse your partner of something that hasn't actually occurred. It can also take the form of nitpicking and being very critical of a partner. Your trust in your partner would lack day by day, and you would find yourself drifting apart from them.

5. Difficulties with Physical Contact

Fear of intimacy can lead to extremes when it comes to physical contact. It would swing between having a constant need for physical contact or avoiding it entirely. You might be inattentive to your partner's needs and solely concentrate on your own need for sexual release or gratification. People with a fear of intimacy may also recoil from sex altogether. Both ends of the spectrum lead to an inability to let go or communicate intimately emotionally. Letting yourself be emotionally naked and bringing up your fears and insecurities to your partner may help you overcome this problem.

6. You're Angry - A Lot

One way that the deep, subconscious fear of intimacy can manifest is via anger. Constant explosions of anger might indicate immaturity, and immature people are not able to form intimate relationships. Everyone gets angry sometimes, and it's an emotion that we cannot ignore, even if we want to. But if you find that your feelings of anger bubble up constantly or inappropriately, a fear of intimacy may be lurking underneath. Don't deny these intimacy issues, but instead put them on the table and communicate effectively with the person you are interested in.

Conclusion

Actions that root out in fear of intimacy only perpetuate the concern. With effort, especially a good therapist, many people have overcome this fear and developed the understanding and tools needed to create a long-term intimate relationship.

CPSIA information can be obtained
at www.ICGtesting.com
Printed in the USA
LVHW082356150122
708614LV00013B/435